Catholic Gospel Readings
of the Sunday Masses
USA
A. D. 2022

Catholic Gospel Readings
of the Sunday Masses
USA
A. D. 2022

Bibliografische Information der Deutschen Nationalbibliothek: Die Deutsche Nationalbibliothek verzeichnet diese Publikation in der Deutschen Nationalbibliografie; detaillierte bibliografische Daten sind im Internet über dnb.dnb.de abrufbar.

Bibliographic information of the German National Library: The German National Library lists this publication in the German National Bibliography; detailed bibliographic data are available on the Internet at dnb.dnb.de.

Herstellung und Verlag: BoD – Books on Demand, Norderstedt, Germany

ISBN: 9783755711568

Table of contents

Introduction

In this book you will find the Sunday Gospel readings for the year 2022. So this book accompanies you through the whole year. As an aid for your prayer at home or also for all those who cannot participate in the sunday mass for professional or health reasons.

Additionally included are the Gospel readings for New Year's Day (Solemnity of Mary),
Day of Prayer for the Legal Protection of Unborn Children,
Holy Thursday,
Good Friday,
Holy Saturday,
Ascension of the Lord,
The Immaculate Heart of the Blessed Virgin Mary,
The Immaculate Conception of the Blessed Virgin Mary,
Christmas Eve,
The Holy Family,
New Year's Eve,

and important prayers in Latin and English language.

May the Lord bless you and be with you always.

All Bible quotations are taken from the public domain World English Bible.

January

Saturday, January 1ˢᵗ, 2022
Solemnity of Mary, The Holy Mother of God

They came with haste, and found both Mary and Joseph, and the baby was lying in the feeding trough. When they saw it, they publicized widely the saying which was spoken to them about this child. All who heard it wondered at the things which were spoken to them by the shepherds. But Mary kept all these sayings, pondering them in her heart. The shepherds returned, glorifying and praising God for all the things that they had heard and seen, just as it was told them.

When eight days were fulfilled for the circumcision of the child, his name was called Jesus, which was given by the angel before he was conceived in the womb.

Luke 2: 16 – 21

Sunday, January 2nd, 2022
The Epiphany of the Lord

Now when Jesus was born in Bethlehem of Judea in the days of King Herod, behold, wise men from the east came to Jerusalem, saying, "Where is he who is born King of the Jews? For we saw his star in the east, and have come to worship him." When King Herod heard it, he was troubled, and all Jerusalem with him. Gathering together all the chief priests and scribes of the people, he asked them where the Christ would be born. They said to him, "In Bethlehem of Judea, for this is written through the prophet,

'You Bethlehem, land of Judah,
are in no way least among the princes of Judah;
for out of you shall come a governor
who shall shepherd my people, Israel.'"

Then Herod secretly called the wise men, and learned from them exactly what time the star appeared. He sent them to Bethlehem, and said, "Go and search diligently for the young child. When you have found him, bring me word, so that I also may come and worship him."

They, having heard the king, went their way; and behold, the star, which they saw in the east, went before them until it came and stood over where the young child was. When they saw the star, they rejoiced with exceedingly great joy. They came into

11

the house and saw the young child with Mary, his mother, and they fell down and worshiped him. Opening their treasures, they offered to him gifts: gold, frankincense, and myrrh. Being warned in a dream not to return to Herod, they went back to their own country another way.

Matthew 2: 1 – 12

Sunday, January 9th, 2022
The Baptism of the Lord

As the people were in expectation, and all men reasoned in their hearts concerning John, whether perhaps he was the Christ, John answered them all, "I indeed baptize you with water, but he comes who is mightier than I, the strap of whose sandals I am not worthy to loosen. He will baptize you in the Holy Spirit and fire,

(…)

Now when all the people were baptized, Jesus also had been baptized, and was praying. The sky was opened, and the Holy Spirit descended in a bodily form like a dove on him; and a voice came out of the sky, saying "You are my beloved Son. In you I am well pleased."

Luke 3: 15 – 16, 21 – 22

13

The third day, there was a wedding in Cana of Galilee. Jesus' mother was there. Jesus also was invited, with his disciples, to the wedding. When the wine ran out, Jesus' mother said to him, "They have no wine."

Jesus said to her, "Woman, what does that have to do with you and me? My hour has not yet come."

His mother said to the servants, "Whatever he says to you, do it." Now there were six water pots of stone set there after the Jews' way of purifying, containing two or three metretes apiece. Jesus said to them, "Fill the water pots with water." So they filled them up to the brim. He said to them, "Now draw some out, and take it to the ruler of the feast." So they took it. When the ruler of the feast tasted the water now become wine, and didn't know where it came from (but the servants who had drawn the water knew), the ruler of the feast called the bridegroom and said to him, "Everyone serves the good wine first, and when the guests have drunk freely, then that which is worse. You have kept the good wine until now!" This beginning of his signs Jesus did in Cana of Galilee, and revealed his glory; and his disciples believed in him.

John 2: 1 – 11

Saturday, January 22nd, 2022
Day of Prayer for the Legal Protection of Unborn Children

The multitude came together again, so that they could not so much as eat bread. When his friends heard it, they went out to seize him; for they said, "He is insane."

Mark 3: 20 – 21

15

Since many have undertaken to set in order a narrative concerning those matters which have been fulfilled among us, even as those who from the beginning were eyewitnesses and servants of the word delivered them to us, it seemed good to me also, having traced the course of all things accurately from the first, to write to you in order, most excellent Theophilus; that you might know the certainty concerning the things in which you were instructed.

(...)

Jesus returned in the power of the Spirit into Galilee, and news about him spread through all the surrounding area. He taught in their synagogues, being glorified by all.

He came to Nazareth, where he had been brought up. He entered, as was his custom, into the synagogue on the Sabbath day, and stood up to read. The book of the prophet Isaiah was handed to him. He opened the book, and found the place where it was written,

"The Spirit of the Lord is on me,
because he has anointed me to preach good news to the poor.
He has sent me to heal the broken hearted,
to proclaim release to the captives,

recovering of sight to the blind,

to deliver those who are crushed,

and to proclaim the acceptable year of the Lord."

He closed the book, gave it back to the attendant, and sat down. The eyes of all in the synagogue were fastened on him. He began to tell them, "Today, this Scripture has been fulfilled in your hearing."

Luke 1, 1 – 4; 4, 14 – 21

He began to tell them, "Today, this Scripture has been fulfilled in your hearing."

All testified about him, and wondered at the gracious words which proceeded out of his mouth, and they said, "Isn't this Joseph's son?"

He said to them, "Doubtless you will tell me this parable, 'Physician, heal yourself! Whatever we have heard done at Capernaum, do also here in your hometown.'" He said, "Most certainly I tell you, no prophet is acceptable in his hometown. But truly I tell you, there were many widows in Israel in the days of Elijah, when the sky was shut up three years and six months, when a great famine came over all the land. Elijah was sent to none of them, except to Zarephath, in the land of Sidon, to a woman who was a widow. There were many lepers in Israel in the time of Elisha the prophet, yet not one of them was cleansed, except Naaman, the Syrian."

They were all filled with wrath in the synagogue, as they heard these things. They rose up, threw him out of the city, and led him to the brow of the hill that their city was built on, that they might throw him off the cliff. But he, passing through the middle of them, went his way.

Luke 4: 21 – 30

February

Now while the multitude pressed on him and heard the word of God, he was standing by the lake of Gennesaret. He saw two boats standing by the lake, but the fishermen had gone out of them, and were washing their nets. He entered into one of the boats, which was Simon's, and asked him to put out a little from the land. He sat down and taught the multitudes from the boat. When he had finished speaking, he said to Simon, "Put out into the deep, and let down your nets for a catch."

Simon answered him, "Master, we worked all night, and took nothing; but at your word I will let down the net." When they had done this, they caught a great multitude of fish, and their net was breaking. They beckoned to their partners in the other boat, that they should come and help them. They came, and filled both boats, so that they began to sink. But Simon Peter, when he saw it, fell down at Jesus' knees, saying, "Depart from me, for I am a sinful man, Lord." For he was amazed, and all who were with him, at the catch of fish which they had caught; and so also were James and John, sons of Zebedee, who were partners with Simon.

Jesus said to Simon, "Don't be afraid. From now on you will be catching people alive."

When they had brought their boats to land, they left everything, and followed him.

Luke 5: 1 – 11

Sunday, February 13th, 2022

He came down with them, and stood on a level place, with a crowd of his disciples, and a great number of the people from all Judea and Jerusalem, and the sea coast of Tyre and Sidon, who came to hear him and to be healed of their diseases;

(…)

He lifted up his eyes to his disciples, and said,

"Blessed are you who are poor,
God's Kingdom is yours.
Blessed are you who hunger now,
for you will be filled.
Blessed are you who weep now,
for you will laugh.
Blessed are you when men hate you, and when they exclude
and mock you, and throw out your name as evil, for the Son of
Man's sake.
Rejoice in that day, and leap for joy, for behold, your reward is
great in heaven, for their fathers did the same thing to the
prophets.

"But woe to you who are rich!
For you have received your consolation.
Woe to you, you who are full now,

21

for you will be hungry.

Woe to you who laugh now,

for you will mourn and weep.

Woe, when men speak well of you,

for their fathers did the same thing to the false prophets.

Luke 6: 17, 20 – 26

Sunday, February 20th, 2022

"But I tell you who hear: love your enemies, do good to those who hate you, bless those who curse you, and pray for those who mistreat you. To him who strikes you on the cheek, offer also the other; and from him who takes away your cloak, don't withhold your coat also. Give to everyone who asks you, and don't ask him who takes away your goods to give them back again.

"As you would like people to do to you, do exactly so to them. If you love those who love you, what credit is that to you? For even sinners love those who love them. If you do good to those who do good to you, what credit is that to you? For even sinners do the same. If you lend to those from whom you hope to receive, what credit is that to you? Even sinners lend to sinners, to receive back as much. But love your enemies, and do good, and lend, expecting nothing back; and your reward will be great, and you will be children of the Most High; for he is kind toward the unthankful and evil.

"Therefore be merciful,
even as your Father is also merciful.
Don't judge,
and you won't be judged.
Don't condemn,
and you won't be condemned.

23

Set free,

and you will be set free.

"Give, and it will be given to you: good measure, pressed down, shaken together, and running over, will be given to you. For with the same measure you measure it will be measured back to you."

Luke 6: 27 – 38

Sunday, February 27th, 2022

He spoke a parable to them. "Can the blind guide the blind? Won't they both fall into a pit? A disciple is not above his teacher, but everyone when he is fully trained will be like his teacher. Why do you see the speck of chaff that is in your brother's eye, but don't consider the beam that is in your own eye? Or how can you tell your brother, 'Brother, let me remove the speck of chaff that is in your eye,' when you yourself don't see the beam that is in your own eye? You hypocrite! First remove the beam from your own eye, and then you can see clearly to remove the speck of chaff that is in your brother's eye. For there is no good tree that produces rotten fruit; nor again a rotten tree that produces good fruit. For each tree is known by its own fruit. For people don't gather figs from thorns, nor do they gather grapes from a bramble bush. The good man out of the good treasure of his heart brings out that which is good, and the evil man out of the evil treasure of his heart brings out that which is evil, for out of the abundance of the heart, his mouth speaks.

Luke 6. 39 – 45

March

Sunday, March 6th, 2022

Jesus, full of the Holy Spirit, returned from the Jordan, and was led by the Spirit into the wilderness for forty days, being tempted by the devil. He ate nothing in those days. Afterward, when they were completed, he was hungry. The devil said to him, "If you are the Son of God, command this stone to become bread."

Jesus answered him, saying, "It is written, 'Man shall not live by bread alone, but by every word of God.'"

The devil, leading him up on a high mountain, showed him all the kingdoms of the world in a moment of time. The devil said to him, "I will give you all this authority, and their glory, for it has been delivered to me; and I give it to whomever I want. If you therefore will worship before me, it will all be yours."

Jesus answered him, "Get behind me Satan! For it is written, 'You shall worship the Lord your God, and you shall serve him only.'"

He led him to Jerusalem, and set him on the pinnacle of the temple, and said to him, "If you are the Son of God, cast yourself down from here, for it is written,

'He will put his angels in charge of you, to guard you;'

and,

'On their hands they will bear you up,

28

lest perhaps you dash your foot against a stone.'"

Jesus answering, said to him, "It has been said, 'You shall not tempt the Lord your God.'"

When the devil had completed every temptation, he departed from him until another time.

Luke 4: 1 – 13

Sunday, March 13ᵗʰ, 2022

About eight days after these sayings, he took with him Peter, John, and James, and went up onto the mountain to pray. As he was praying, the appearance of his face was altered, and his clothing became white and dazzling. Behold, two men were talking with him, who were Moses and Elijah, who appeared in glory, and spoke of his departure, which he was about to accomplish at Jerusalem.

Now Peter and those who were with him were heavy with sleep, but when they were fully awake, they saw his glory, and the two men who stood with him. As they were parting from him, Peter said to Jesus, "Master, it is good for us to be here. Let's make three tents: one for you, one for Moses, and one for Elijah," not knowing what he said.

While he said these things, a cloud came and overshadowed them, and they were afraid as they entered into the cloud. A voice came out of the cloud, saying, "This is my beloved Son. Listen to him!" When the voice came, Jesus was found alone. They were silent, and told no one in those days any of the things which they had seen.

Luke 9: 28 – 36

Now there were some present at the same time who told him about the Galileans, whose blood Pilate had mixed with their sacrifices. Jesus answered them, "Do you think that these Galileans were worse sinners than all the other Galileans, because they suffered such things? I tell you, no, but unless you repent, you will all perish in the same way. Or those eighteen, on whom the tower in Siloam fell and killed them; do you think that they were worse offenders than all the men who dwell in Jerusalem? I tell you, no, but, unless you repent, you will all perish in the same way."

He spoke this parable. "A certain man had a fig tree planted in his vineyard, and he came seeking fruit on it, and found none. He said to the vine dresser, 'Behold, these three years I have come looking for fruit on this fig tree, and found none. Cut it down. Why does it waste the soil?' He answered, 'Lord, leave it alone this year also, until I dig around it and fertilize it. If it bears fruit, fine; but if not, after that, you can cut it down.'"

Luke 13: 1 – 9

Now all the tax collectors and sinners were coming close to him to hear him. The Pharisees and the scribes murmured, saying, "This man welcomes sinners, and eats with them."

He told them this parable.

(…)

He said, "A certain man had two sons. The younger of them said to his father, 'Father, give me my share of your property.' So he divided his livelihood between them. Not many days after, the younger son gathered all of this together and traveled into a far country. There he wasted his property with riotous living. When he had spent all of it, there arose a severe famine in that country, and he began to be in need. He went and joined himself to one of the citizens of that country, and he sent him into his fields to feed pigs. He wanted to fill his belly with the husks that the pigs ate, but no one gave him any. But when he came to himself he said, 'How many hired servants of my father's have bread enough to spare, and I'm dying with hunger! I will get up and go to my father, and will tell him, "Father, I have sinned against heaven, and in your sight. I am no more worthy to be called your son. Make me as one of your hired servants."'

"He arose, and came to his father. But while he was still far off, his father saw him, and was moved with compassion, and ran, and fell on his neck, and kissed him. The son said to him, 'Father, I have sinned against heaven and in your sight. I am no longer worthy to be called your son.'

"But the father said to his servants, 'Bring out the best robe, and put it on him. Put a ring on his hand, and sandals on his feet. Bring the fattened calf, kill it, and let's eat, and celebrate; for this, my son, was dead, and is alive again. He was lost, and is found.' Then they began to celebrate.

"Now his elder son was in the field. As he came near to the house, he heard music and dancing. He called one of the servants to him, and asked what was going on. He said to him, 'Your brother has come, and your father has killed the fattened calf, because he has received him back safe and healthy.' But he was angry, and would not go in. Therefore his father came out, and begged him. But he answered his father, 'Behold, these many years I have served you, and I never disobeyed a commandment of yours, but you never gave me a goat, that I might celebrate with my friends. But when this your son came, who has devoured your living with prostitutes, you killed the fattened calf for him.'

"He said to him, 'Son, you are always with me, and all that is mine is yours. But it was appropriate to celebrate and be glad, for this, your brother, was dead, and is alive again. He was lost, and is found.'"

Luke 15: 1 – 3, 11 – 32

April

but Jesus went to the Mount of Olives. Now very early in the morning, he came again into the temple, and all the people came to him. He sat down and taught them. The scribes and the Pharisees brought a woman taken in adultery. Having set her in the middle, they told him, "Teacher, we found this woman in adultery, in the very act. Now in our law, Moses commanded us to stone such women. What then do you say about her?" They said this testing him, that they might have something to accuse him of.

But Jesus stooped down and wrote on the ground with his finger. But when they continued asking him, he looked up and said to them, "He who is without sin among you, let him throw the first stone at her." Again he stooped down and wrote on the ground with his finger.

They, when they heard it, being convicted by their conscience, went out one by one, beginning from the oldest, even to the last. Jesus was left alone with the woman where she was, in the middle. Jesus, standing up, saw her and said, "Woman, where are your accusers? Did no one condemn you?"

She said, "No one, Lord." Jesus said, "Neither do I condemn you. Go your way. From now on, sin no more."

John 8: 1 – 11

36

Sunday, April 10th, 2022
Palm Sunday of the Passion of the Lord

When the hour had come, he sat down with the twelve apostles. He said to them, "I have earnestly desired to eat this Passover with you before I suffer, for I tell you, I will no longer by any means eat of it until it is fulfilled in God's Kingdom." He received a cup, and when he had given thanks, he said, "Take this, and share it among yourselves, for I tell you, I will not drink at all again from the fruit of the vine, until God's Kingdom comes."

He took bread, and when he had given thanks, he broke, and gave it to them, saying, "This is my body which is given for you. Do this in memory of me." Likewise, he took the cup after supper, saying, "This cup is the new covenant in my blood, which is poured out for you. But behold, the hand of him who betrays me is with me on the table. The Son of Man indeed goes, as it has been determined, but woe to that man through whom he is betrayed!"

They began to question among themselves, which of them it was who would do this thing. A dispute also arose among them, which of them was considered to be greatest. He said to them, "The kings of the nations lord it over them, and those who have authority over them are called 'benefactors.' But not so with you. But one who is the greater among you, let him become as the younger, and one who is governing, as one who serves. For who is greater, one who sits at the table, or one who serves? Isn't it he who sits at the table? But I am among you as one who serves. But you are those who have continued with me in my trials. I confer on you a kingdom, even as my Father conferred on me, that you may eat and drink at my table in my Kingdom. You will sit on thrones, judging the twelve tribes of Israel."

The Lord said, "Simon, Simon, behold, Satan asked to have all of you, that he might sift you as wheat, but I prayed for you, that your faith wouldn't fail. You, when once you have turned again, establish your brothers."

He said to him, "Lord, I am ready to go with you both to prison and to death!"

He said, "I tell you, Peter, the rooster will by no means crow today until you deny that you know me three times."

He said to them, "When I sent you out without purse, wallet, and sandals, did you lack anything?"

They said, "Nothing."

Then he said to them, "But now, whoever has a purse, let him take it, and likewise a wallet. Whoever has none, let him sell his cloak, and buy a sword. For I tell you that this which is written must still be fulfilled in me: 'He was counted with transgressors.' For that which concerns me has an end."

They said, "Lord, behold, here are two swords."

He said to them, "That is enough."

He came out and went, as his custom was, to the Mount of Olives. His disciples also followed him. When he was at the place, he said to them, "Pray that you don't enter into temptation."

He was withdrawn from them about a stone's throw, and he knelt down and prayed, saying, "Father, if you are willing, remove this cup from me. Nevertheless, not my will, but yours, be done."

An angel from heaven appeared to him, strengthening him. Being in agony he prayed more earnestly. His sweat became like great drops of blood falling down on the ground.

When he rose up from his prayer, he came to the disciples, and found them sleeping because of grief, and said to them, "Why do you sleep? Rise and pray that you may not enter into temptation."

While he was still speaking, a crowd appeared. He who was called Judas, one of the twelve, was leading them. He came near to Jesus to kiss him. But Jesus said to him, "Judas, do you betray the Son of Man with a kiss?"

When those who were around him saw what was about to happen, they said to him, "Lord, shall we strike with the sword?" A certain one of them struck the servant of the high priest, and cut off his right ear.

But Jesus answered, "Let me at least do this"—and he touched his ear, and healed him. Jesus said to the chief priests, captains of the temple, and elders, who had come against him, "Have you come out as against a robber, with swords and clubs? When I was with you in the temple daily, you didn't stretch out your hands against me. But this is your hour, and the power of darkness."

They seized him, and led him away, and brought him into the high priest's house. But Peter followed from a distance. When they had kindled a fire in the middle of the courtyard, and had sat down together, Peter sat among them. A certain servant girl saw him as he sat in the light, and looking intently at him, said, "This man also was with him."

He denied Jesus, saying, "Woman, I don't know him."

After a little while someone else saw him, and said, "You also are one of them!"

But Peter answered, "Man, I am not!"

After about one hour passed, another confidently affirmed, saying, "Truly this man also was with him, for he is a Galilean!"

But Peter said, "Man, I don't know what you are talking about!" Immediately, while he was still speaking, a rooster crowed. The Lord turned and looked at Peter. Then Peter remembered the Lord's word, how he said to him, "Before the rooster crows you will deny me three times." He went out, and wept bitterly.

The men who held Jesus mocked him and beat him. Having blindfolded him, they struck him on the face and asked him, "Prophesy! Who is the one who struck you?" They spoke many other things against him, insulting him.

As soon as it was day, the assembly of the elders of the people were gathered together, both chief priests and scribes, and they led him away into their council, saying, "If you are the Christ, tell us."

But he said to them, "If I tell you, you won't believe, and if I ask, you will in no way answer me or let me go. From now on, the Son of Man will be seated at the right hand of the power of God."

They all said, "Are you then the Son of God?"

He said to them, "You say it, because I am."

They said, "Why do we need any more witness? For we ourselves have heard from his own mouth!"

The whole company of them rose up and brought him before Pilate. They began to accuse him, saying, "We found this man perverting the nation, forbidding paying taxes to Caesar, and saying that he himself is Christ, a king."

Pilate asked him, "Are you the King of the Jews?"

He answered him, "So you say."

Pilate said to the chief priests and the multitudes, "I find no basis

41

for a charge against this man."

But they insisted, saying, "He stirs up the people, teaching throughout all Judea, beginning from Galilee even to this place." But when Pilate heard Galilee mentioned, he asked if the man was a Galilean. When he found out that he was in Herod's jurisdiction, he sent him to Herod, who was also in Jerusalem during those days.

Now when Herod saw Jesus, he was exceedingly glad, for he had wanted to see him for a long time, because he had heard many things about him. He hoped to see some miracle done by him. He questioned him with many words, but he gave no answers. The chief priests and the scribes stood, vehemently accusing him. Herod with his soldiers humiliated him and mocked him. Dressing him in luxurious clothing, they sent him back to Pilate. Herod and Pilate became friends with each other that very day, for before that they were enemies with each other.

Pilate called together the chief priests, the rulers, and the people, and said to them, "You brought this man to me as one that perverts the people, and behold, having examined him before you, I found no basis for a charge against this man concerning those things of which you accuse him. Neither has Herod, for I sent you to him, and see, nothing worthy of death has been done by him. I will therefore chastise him and release him."

Now he had to release one prisoner to them at the feast. But they all cried out together, saying, "Away with this man! Release to us Barabbas!"— one who was thrown into prison for a certain revolt in the city, and for murder.

Then Pilate spoke to them again, wanting to release Jesus, but they shouted, saying, "Crucify! Crucify him!"

He said to them the third time, "Why? What evil has this man done? I have found no capital crime in him. I will therefore chastise him and release him." But they were urgent with loud voices, asking that he might be crucified. Their voices and the voices of the chief priests prevailed. Pilate decreed that what they asked for should be done. He released him who had been thrown into prison for insurrection and murder, for whom they asked, but he delivered Jesus up to their will.

When they led him away, they grabbed one Simon of Cyrene, coming from the country, and laid on him the cross, to carry it after Jesus. A great multitude of the people followed him, including women who also mourned and lamented him. But Jesus, turning to them, said, "Daughters of Jerusalem, don't weep for me, but weep for yourselves and for your children. For behold, the days are coming in which they will say, 'Blessed are the barren, the wombs that never bore, and the breasts that never nursed.' Then they will begin to tell the mountains, 'Fall on us!' and tell the hills, 'Cover us.' For if they do these things in the green tree, what will be done in the dry?"

43

There were also others, two criminals, led with him to be put to death. When they came to the place that is called "The Skull", they crucified him there with the criminals, one on the right and the other on the left.

Jesus said, "Father, forgive them, for they don't know what they are doing."

Dividing his garments among them, they cast lots. The people stood watching. The rulers with them also scoffed at him, saying, "He saved others. Let him save himself, if this is the Christ of God, his chosen one!"

The soldiers also mocked him, coming to him and offering him vinegar, and saying, "If you are the King of the Jews, save yourself!"

An inscription was also written over him in letters of Greek, Latin, and Hebrew: "THIS IS THE KING OF THE JEWS."

One of the criminals who was hanged insulted him, saying, "If you are the Christ, save yourself and us!"

But the other answered, and rebuking him said, "Don't you even fear God, seeing you are under the same condemnation? And we indeed justly, for we receive the due reward for our deeds, but this man has done nothing wrong." He said to Jesus, "Lord, remember me when you come into your Kingdom."

Jesus said to him, "Assuredly I tell you, today you will be with me in Paradise."

It was now about the sixth hour, and darkness came over the whole land until the ninth hour. The sun was darkened, and the veil of the temple was torn in two. Jesus, crying with a loud voice, said, "Father, into your hands I commit my spirit!" Having said this, he breathed his last.

When the centurion saw what was done, he glorified God, saying, "Certainly this was a righteous man." All the multitudes that came together to see this, when they saw the things that were done, returned home beating their breasts. All his acquaintances and the women who followed with him from Galilee stood at a distance, watching these things.

Behold, a man named Joseph, who was a member of the council, a good and righteous man (he had not consented to their counsel and deed), from Arimathaea, a city of the Jews, who was also waiting for God's Kingdom: this man went to Pilate, and asked for Jesus' body. He took it down, and wrapped it in a linen cloth, and laid him in a tomb that was cut in stone, where no one had ever been laid. It was the day of the Preparation, and the Sabbath was drawing near. The women, who had come with him out of Galilee, followed after, and saw the tomb, and how his body was laid. They returned and prepared spices and ointments. On the Sabbath they rested according to the commandment.

Luke 22: 14 – 23: 56

Thursday, April 14th, 2022
Holy Thursday

Now before the feast of the Passover, Jesus, knowing that his time had come that he would depart from this world to the Father, having loved his own who were in the world, he loved them to the end. During supper, the devil having already put into the heart of Judas Iscariot, Simon's son, to betray him, Jesus, knowing that the Father had given all things into his hands, and that he came from God, and was going to God, arose from supper, and laid aside his outer garments. He took a towel and wrapped a towel around his waist. Then he poured water into the basin, and began to wash the disciples' feet and to wipe them with the towel that was wrapped around him. Then he came to Simon Peter. He said to him, "Lord, do you wash my feet?"

Jesus answered him, "You don't know what I am doing now, but you will understand later."

Peter said to him, "You will never wash my feet!"

Jesus answered him, "If I don't wash you, you have no part with me."

Simon Peter said to him, "Lord, not my feet only, but also my hands and my head!"

Jesus said to him, "Someone who has bathed only needs to have his feet washed, but is completely clean. You are clean, but not all of you." For he knew him who would betray him, therefore he said, "You are not all clean." So when he had washed their feet, put his outer garment back on, and sat down again, he said to them, "Do you know what I have done to you? You call me, 'Teacher' and 'Lord.' You say so correctly, for so I am. If I then, the Lord and the Teacher, have washed your feet, you also ought to wash one another's feet. For I have given you an example, that you should also do as I have done to you.

John 13: 1 – 15

Friday, April 15th, 2022
Good Friday, Friday of the Passion of the Lord

When Jesus had spoken these words, he went out with his disciples over the brook Kidron, where there was a garden, into which he and his disciples entered. Now Judas, who betrayed him, also knew the place, for Jesus often met there with his disciples. Judas then, having taken a detachment of soldiers and officers from the chief priests and the Pharisees, came there with lanterns, torches, and weapons. Jesus therefore, knowing all the things that were happening to him, went out, and said to them, "Who are you looking for?"

They answered him, "Jesus of Nazareth."

Jesus said to them, "I am he."

Judas also, who betrayed him, was standing with them. When therefore he said to them, "I am he," they went backward, and fell to the ground.

Again therefore he asked them, "Who are you looking for?"

They said, "Jesus of Nazareth."

Jesus answered, "I told you that I am he. If therefore you seek me, let these go their way," that the word might be fulfilled which he spoke, "Of those whom you have given me, I have lost none."

Simon Peter therefore, having a sword, drew it, struck the high priest's servant, and cut off his right ear. The servant's name was Malchus. Jesus therefore said to Peter, "Put the sword into its sheath. The cup which the Father has given me, shall I not surely drink it?"

So the detachment, the commanding officer, and the officers of the Jews seized Jesus and bound him, and led him to Annas first, for he was father-in-law to Caiaphas, who was high priest that year. Now it was Caiaphas who advised the Jews that it was expedient that one man should perish for the people. Simon Peter followed Jesus, as did another disciple. Now that disciple was known to the high priest, and entered in with Jesus into the court of the high priest; but Peter was standing at the door outside. So the other disciple, who was known to the high priest, went out and spoke to her who kept the door, and brought in Peter. Then the maid who kept the door said to Peter, "Are you also one of this man's disciples?"

He said, "I am not."

Now the servants and the officers were standing there, having made a fire of coals, for it was cold. They were warming themselves. Peter was with them, standing and warming himself. The high priest therefore asked Jesus about his disciples and about his teaching. Jesus answered him, "I spoke openly to the world. I always taught in synagogues, and in the temple, where the Jews always meet. I said nothing in secret. Why do you ask me? Ask those who have heard me what I said to them.

Behold, they know the things which I said."

When he had said this, one of the officers standing by slapped Jesus with his hand, saying, "Do you answer the high priest like that?"

Jesus answered him, "If I have spoken evil, testify of the evil; but if well, why do you beat me?"

Annas sent him bound to Caiaphas, the high priest. Now Simon Peter was standing and warming himself. They said therefore to him, "You aren't also one of his disciples, are you?"

He denied it and said, "I am not."

One of the servants of the high priest, being a relative of him whose ear Peter had cut off, said, "Didn't I see you in the garden with him?"

Peter therefore denied it again, and immediately the rooster crowed.

They led Jesus therefore from Caiaphas into the Praetorium. It was early, and they themselves didn't enter into the Praetorium, that they might not be defiled, but might eat the Passover. Pilate therefore went out to them, and said, "What accusation do you bring against this man?"

They answered him, "If this man weren't an evildoer, we wouldn't have delivered him up to you."

Pilate therefore said to them, "Take him yourselves, and judge him according to your law."

Therefore the Jews said to him, "It is illegal for us to put anyone to death," that the word of Jesus might be fulfilled, which he spoke, signifying by what kind of death he should die.

Pilate therefore entered again into the Praetorium, called Jesus, and said to him, "Are you the King of the Jews?"

Jesus answered him, "Do you say this by yourself, or did others tell you about me?"

Pilate answered, "I'm not a Jew, am I? Your own nation and the chief priests delivered you to me. What have you done?"

Jesus answered, "My Kingdom is not of this world. If my Kingdom were of this world, then my servants would fight, that I wouldn't be delivered to the Jews. But now my Kingdom is not from here."

Pilate therefore said to him, "Are you a king then?"

Jesus answered, "You say that I am a king. For this reason I have been born, and for this reason I have come into the world, that I should testify to the truth. Everyone who is of the truth listens to my voice."

Pilate said to him, "What is truth?"

When he had said this, he went out again to the Jews, and said to them, "I find no basis for a charge against him. But you have a custom, that I should release someone to you at the Passover.

51

Therefore, do you want me to release to you the King of the Jews?"

Then they all shouted again, saying, "Not this man, but Barabbas!" Now Barabbas was a robber.

So Pilate then took Jesus, and flogged him. The soldiers twisted thorns into a crown, and put it on his head, and dressed him in a purple garment. They kept saying, "Hail, King of the Jews!" and they kept slapping him.

Then Pilate went out again, and said to them, "Behold, I bring him out to you, that you may know that I find no basis for a charge against him."

Jesus therefore came out, wearing the crown of thorns and the purple garment. Pilate said to them, "Behold, the man!"

When therefore the chief priests and the officers saw him, they shouted, saying, "Crucify! Crucify!"

Pilate said to them, "Take him yourselves, and crucify him, for I find no basis for a charge against him."

The Jews answered him, "We have a law, and by our law he ought to die, because he made himself the Son of God."

When therefore Pilate heard this saying, he was more afraid. He entered into the Praetorium again, and said to Jesus, "Where are you from?" But Jesus gave him no answer. Pilate therefore said to him, "Aren't you speaking to me? Don't you know that I have power to release you and have power to crucify you?"

Jesus answered, "You would have no power at all against me, unless it were given to you from above. Therefore he who delivered me to you has greater sin."

At this, Pilate was seeking to release him, but the Jews cried out, saying, "If you release this man, you aren't Caesar's friend! Everyone who makes himself a king speaks against Caesar!"

When Pilate therefore heard these words, he brought Jesus out and sat down on the judgment seat at a place called "The Pavement", but in Hebrew, "Gabbatha." Now it was the Preparation Day of the Passover, at about the sixth hour. He said to the Jews, "Behold, your King!"

They cried out, "Away with him! Away with him! Crucify him!"

Pilate said to them, "Shall I crucify your King?"

The chief priests answered, "We have no king but Caesar!"

So then he delivered him to them to be crucified. So they took Jesus and led him away. He went out, bearing his cross, to the place called "The Place of a Skull", which is called in Hebrew, "Golgotha", where they crucified him, and with him two others, on either side one, and Jesus in the middle. Pilate wrote a title also, and put it on the cross. There was written, "JESUS OF NAZARETH, THE KING OF THE JEWS." Therefore many of the Jews read this title, for the place where Jesus was crucified was near the city; and it was written in Hebrew, in Latin, and in

Greek. The chief priests of the Jews therefore said to Pilate, "Don't write, 'The King of the Jews,' but, 'he said, "I am King of the Jews."'"

Pilate answered, "What I have written, I have written."

Then the soldiers, when they had crucified Jesus, took his garments and made four parts, to every soldier a part; and also the coat. Now the coat was without seam, woven from the top throughout. Then they said to one another, "Let's not tear it, but cast lots for it to decide whose it will be," that the Scripture might be fulfilled, which says,

"They parted my garments among them.
For my cloak they cast lots."

Therefore the soldiers did these things.

But standing by Jesus' cross were his mother, his mother's sister, Mary the wife of Clopas, and Mary Magdalene. Therefore when Jesus saw his mother, and the disciple whom he loved standing there, he said to his mother, "Woman, behold, your son!" Then he said to the disciple, "Behold, your mother!" From that hour, the disciple took her to his own home.

After this, Jesus, seeing that all things were now finished, that the Scripture might be fulfilled, said, "I am thirsty." Now a vessel full of vinegar was set there; so they put a sponge full of the vinegar on hyssop, and held it at his mouth. When Jesus therefore had received the vinegar, he said, "It is finished." Then he bowed his head, and gave up his spirit.

Therefore the Jews, because it was the Preparation Day, so that the bodies wouldn't remain on the cross on the Sabbath (for that Sabbath was a special one), asked of Pilate that their legs might be broken, and that they might be taken away. Therefore the soldiers came, and broke the legs of the first, and of the other who was crucified with him; but when they came to Jesus, and saw that he was already dead, they didn't break his legs. However one of the soldiers pierced his side with a spear, and immediately blood and water came out. He who has seen has testified, and his testimony is true. He knows that he tells the truth, that you may believe. For these things happened that the Scripture might be fulfilled, "A bone of him will not be broken."Again another Scripture says, "They will look on him whom they pierced."

After these things, Joseph of Arimathaea, being a disciple of Jesus, but secretly for fear of the Jews, asked of Pilate that he might take away Jesus' body. Pilate gave him permission. He came therefore and took away his body. Nicodemus, who at first came to Jesus by night, also came bringing a mixture of myrrh and aloes, about a hundred Roman pounds.So they took Jesus' body, and bound it in linen cloths with the spices, as the custom of the Jews is to bury. Now in the place where he was crucified there was a garden. In the garden was a new tomb in which no man had ever yet been laid. Then because of the Jews'

Preparation Day (for the tomb was near at hand) they laid Jesus there.

John 18: 1 – 19: 42

Saturday, April 16th, 2022
Holy Saturday

But on the first day of the week, at early dawn, they and some others came to the tomb, bringing the spices which they had prepared. They found the stone rolled away from the tomb. They entered in, and didn't find the Lord Jesus' body. While they were greatly perplexed about this, behold, two men stood by them in dazzling clothing. Becoming terrified, they bowed their faces down to the earth.

They said to them, "Why do you seek the living among the dead? He isn't here, but is risen. Remember what he told you when he was still in Galilee, saying that the Son of Man must be delivered up into the hands of sinful men and be crucified, and the third day rise again?"

They remembered his words, returned from the tomb, and told all these things to the eleven and to all the rest. Now they were Mary Magdalene, Joanna, and Mary the mother of James. The other women with them told these things to the apostles. These words seemed to them to be nonsense, and they didn't believe them. But Peter got up and ran to the tomb. Stooping and looking in, he saw the strips of linen lying by themselves, and he departed to his home, wondering what had happened.

Luke 24: 1 – 12

Sunday, April 17th, 2022
Easter Sunday of the Resurrection of the Lord

Now on the first day of the week, Mary Magdalene went early, while it was still dark, to the tomb, and saw the stone taken away from the tomb. Therefore she ran and came to Simon Peter and to the other disciple whom Jesus loved, and said to them, "They have taken away the Lord out of the tomb, and we don't know where they have laid him!"

Therefore Peter and the other disciple went out, and they went toward the tomb. They both ran together. The other disciple outran Peter, and came to the tomb first. Stooping and looking in, he saw the linen cloths lying, yet he didn't enter in. Then Simon Peter came, following him, and entered into the tomb. He saw the linen cloths lying, and the cloth that had been on his head, not lying with the linen cloths, but rolled up in a place by itself. So then the other disciple who came first to the tomb also entered in, and he saw and believed. For as yet they didn't know the Scripture, that he must rise from the dead.

John 20: 1 – 9

Sunday, April 24th, 2022
Sunday of Divine Mercy

When therefore it was evening on that day, the first day of the week, and when the doors were locked where the disciples were assembled, for fear of the Jews, Jesus came and stood in the middle, and said to them, "Peace be to you."

When he had said this, he showed them his hands and his side. The disciples therefore were glad when they saw the Lord. Jesus therefore said to them again, "Peace be to you. As the Father has sent me, even so I send you." When he had said this, he breathed on them, and said to them, "Receive the Holy Spirit! If you forgive anyone's sins, they have been forgiven them. If you retain anyone's sins, they have been retained."

But Thomas, one of the twelve, called Didymus, wasn't with them when Jesus came. The other disciples therefore said to him, "We have seen the Lord!"

But he said to them, "Unless I see in his hands the print of the nails, put my finger into the print of the nails, and put my hand into his side, I will not believe."

After eight days again his disciples were inside and Thomas was with them. Jesus came, the doors being locked, and stood in the middle, and said, "Peace be to you." Then he said to Thomas, "Reach here your finger, and see my hands. Reach here your hand, and put it into my side. Don't be unbelieving, but

59

believing."

Thomas answered him, "My Lord and my God!"

Jesus said to him, "Because you have seen me, you have believed. Blessed are those who have not seen, and have believed."

Therefore Jesus did many other signs in the presence of his disciples, which are not written in this book; but these are written, that you may believe that Jesus is the Christ, the Son of God, and that believing you may have life in his name.

John 20: 19 – 31

May

After these things, Jesus revealed himself again to the disciples at the sea of Tiberias. He revealed himself this way. Simon Peter, Thomas called Didymus, Nathanael of Cana in Galilee, and the sons of Zebedee, and two others of his disciples were together. Simon Peter said to them, "I'm going fishing."

They told him, "We are also coming with you." They immediately went out, and entered into the boat. That night, they caught nothing. But when day had already come, Jesus stood on the beach, yet the disciples didn't know that it was Jesus. Jesus therefore said to them, "Children, have you anything to eat?"

They answered him, "No."

He said to them, "Cast the net on the right side of the boat, and you will find some."

They cast it therefore, and now they weren't able to draw it in for the multitude of fish. That disciple therefore whom Jesus loved said to Peter, "It's the Lord!"

So when Simon Peter heard that it was the Lord, he wrapped his coat around himself (for he was naked), and threw himself into the sea. But the other disciples came in the little boat (for they were not far from the land, but about two hundred cubits away), dragging the net full of fish. So when they got out on the land, they saw a fire of coals there, with fish and bread laid on it. Jesus said to them, "Bring some of the fish which you have just caught."

Simon Peter went up, and drew the net to land, full of one hundred fifty-three great fish. Even though there were so many, the net wasn't torn.

Jesus said to them, "Come and eat breakfast!"

None of the disciples dared inquire of him, "Who are you?" knowing that it was the Lord.

Then Jesus came and took the bread, gave it to them, and the fish likewise. This is now the third time that Jesus was revealed to his disciples after he had risen from the dead. So when they had eaten their breakfast, Jesus said to Simon Peter, "Simon, son of Jonah, do you love me more than these?"

He said to him, "Yes, Lord; you know that I have affection for you."

He said to him, "Feed my lambs." He said to him again a second time, "Simon, son of Jonah, do you love me?"

He said to him, "Yes, Lord; you know that I have affection for you."

He said to him, "Tend my sheep." He said to him the third time, "Simon, son of Jonah, do you have affection for me?"

Peter was grieved because he asked him the third time, "Do you have affection for me?" He said to him, "Lord, you know everything. You know that I have affection for you."

Jesus said to him, "Feed my sheep. Most certainly I tell you, when you were young, you dressed yourself and walked where you wanted to. But when you are old, you will stretch out your hands, and another will dress you and carry you where you don't want to go."

Now he said this, signifying by what kind of death he would glorify God. When he had said this, he said to him, "Follow me."

John 21, 1 – 19

Sunday, May 8th, 2022

My sheep hear my voice, and I know them, and they follow me. I give eternal life to them. They will never perish, and no one will snatch them out of my hand. My Father who has given them to me is greater than all. No one is able to snatch them out of my Father's hand. I and the Father are one."

John 10: 27 – 30

When he had gone out, Jesus said, "Now the Son of Man has been glorified, and God has been glorified in him. If God has been glorified in him, God will also glorify him in himself, and he will glorify him immediately. Little children, I will be with you a little while longer. You will seek me, and as I said to the Jews, 'Where I am going, you can't come,' so now I tell you. A new commandment I give to you, that you love one another. Just as I have loved you, you also love one another. By this everyone will know that you are my disciples, if you have love for one another."

John 13: 31 – 35

Sunday, May 22nd, 2022

Jesus answered him, "If a man loves me, he will keep my word. My Father will love him, and we will come to him, and make our home with him. He who doesn't love me doesn't keep my words. The word which you hear isn't mine, but the Father's who sent me. I have said these things to you while still living with you. But the Counselor, the Holy Spirit, whom the Father will send in my name, will teach you all things, and will remind you of all that I said to you. Peace I leave with you. My peace I give to you; not as the world gives, I give to you. Don't let your heart be troubled, neither let it be fearful. You heard how I told you, 'I go away, and I come to you.' If you loved me, you would have rejoiced, because I said 'I am going to my Father;' for the Father is greater than I. Now I have told you before it happens so that when it happens, you may believe.

John 14: 23 - 29

Thursday, May 26th, 2022,
(The Ascension of the Lord
in New York, Boston, Philadelphia, Omaha,
Hartford and Newark;
see May 29th)

Sunday, May 29th, 2022
The Ascension of the Lord

He said to them, "Thus it is written, and thus it was necessary for the Christ to suffer and to rise from the dead the third day, and that repentance and remission of sins should be preached in his name to all the nations, beginning at Jerusalem. You are witnesses of these things. Behold, I send out the promise of my Father on you. But wait in the city of Jerusalem until you are clothed with power from on high."

He led them out as far as Bethany, and he lifted up his hands, and blessed them. While he blessed them, he withdrew from them, and was carried up into heaven. They worshiped him, and returned to Jerusalem with great joy, and were continually in the temple, praising and blessing God. Amen.

Luke 24: 46 – 53

June

Sunday, June 05th, 2022
Pentecost Sunday

When therefore it was evening on that day, the first day of the week, and when the doors were locked where the disciples were assembled, for fear of the Jews, Jesus came and stood in the middle, and said to them, "Peace be to you."

When he had said this, he showed them his hands and his side. The disciples therefore were glad when they saw the Lord. Jesus therefore said to them again, "Peace be to you. As the Father has sent me, even so I send you." When he had said this, he breathed on them, and said to them, "Receive the Holy Spirit! If you forgive anyone's sins, they have been forgiven them. If you retain anyone's sins, they have been retained."

John 20: 19 – 23

Sunday, June 12th, 2022
The Most Holy Trinity

"I still have many things to tell you, but you can't bear them now. However when he, the Spirit of truth, has come, he will guide you into all truth, for he will not speak from himself; but whatever he hears, he will speak. He will declare to you things that are coming. He will glorify me, for he will take from what is mine, and will declare it to you. All things that the Father has are mine; therefore I said that he takes of mine and will declare it to you.

John 16: 12 – 15

Sunday, June 19th, 2022
Corpus Christi

But the multitudes, perceiving it, followed him. He welcomed them, spoke to them of God's Kingdom, and he cured those who needed healing. The day began to wear away; and the twelve came and said to him, "Send the multitude away, that they may go into the surrounding villages and farms, and lodge, and get food, for we are here in a deserted place."

But he said to them, "You give them something to eat."

They said, "We have no more than five loaves and two fish, unless we should go and buy food for all these people." For they were about five thousand men.

He said to his disciples, "Make them sit down in groups of about fifty each." They did so, and made them all sit down. He took the five loaves and the two fish, and looking up to the sky, he blessed them, broke them, and gave them to the disciples to set before the multitude. They ate and were all filled. They gathered up twelve baskets of broken pieces that were left over.

Luke 9: 11 – 17

74

Saturday, June 25th, 2022
The Immaculate Heart of the Blessed Virgin Mary

His parents went every year to Jerusalem at the feast of the Passover.

When he was twelve years old, they went up to Jerusalem according to the custom of the feast, and when they had fulfilled the days, as they were returning, the boy Jesus stayed behind in Jerusalem. Joseph and his mother didn't know it, but supposing him to be in the company, they went a day's journey, and they looked for him among their relatives and acquaintances. When they didn't find him, they returned to Jerusalem, looking for him. After three days they found him in the temple, sitting in the middle of the teachers, both listening to them, and asking them questions. All who heard him were amazed at his understanding and his answers. When they saw him, they were astonished, and his mother said to him, "Son, why have you treated us this way? Behold, your father and I were anxiously looking for you."

He said to them, "Why were you looking for me? Didn't you know that I must be in my Father's house?" They didn't understand the saying which he spoke to them. And he went down with them, and came to Nazareth. He was subject to them, and his mother kept all these sayings in her heart.

Luke 2: 41 – 51

75

Sunday, June 26th, 2022

It came to pass, when the days were near that he should be taken up, he intently set his face to go to Jerusalem and sent messengers before his face. They went and entered into a village of the Samaritans, so as to prepare for him. They didn't receive him, because he was traveling with his face set toward Jerusalem. When his disciples, James and John, saw this, they said, "Lord, do you want us to command fire to come down from the sky and destroy them, just as Elijah did?"

But he turned and rebuked them, "You don't know of what kind of spirit you are. For the Son of Man didn't come to destroy men's lives, but to save them."

They went to another village. As they went on the way, a certain man said to him, "I want to follow you wherever you go, Lord."

Jesus said to him, "The foxes have holes, and the birds of the sky have nests, but the Son of Man has no place to lay his head."

He said to another, "Follow me!"

But he said, "Lord, allow me first to go and bury my father."

But Jesus said to him, "Leave the dead to bury their own dead, but you go and announce God's Kingdom."

Another also said, "I want to follow you, Lord, but first allow me to say good-bye to those who are at my house."

76

But Jesus said to him, "No one, having put his hand to the plow and looking back, is fit for God's Kingdom."

Luke 9: 51 – 62

July

Now after these things, the Lord also appointed seventy others, and sent them two by two ahead of him into every city and place where he was about to come. Then he said to them, "The harvest is indeed plentiful, but the laborers are few. Pray therefore to the Lord of the harvest, that he may send out laborers into his harvest. Go your ways. Behold, I send you out as lambs among wolves. Carry no purse, nor wallet, nor sandals. Greet no one on the way. Into whatever house you enter, first say, 'Peace be to this house.' If a son of peace is there, your peace will rest on him; but if not, it will return to you. Remain in that same house, eating and drinking the things they give, for the laborer is worthy of his wages. Don't go from house to house. Into whatever city you enter, and they receive you, eat the things that are set before you. Heal the sick who are there, and tell them, 'God's Kingdom has come near to you.' But into whatever city you enter, and they don't receive you, go out into its streets and say, 'Even the dust from your city that clings to us, we wipe off against you. Nevertheless know this, that God's Kingdom has come near to you.' I tell you, it will be more tolerable in that day for Sodom than for that city.

(…)

The seventy returned with joy, saying, "Lord, even the demons are subject to us in your name!"

He said to them, "I saw Satan having fallen like lightning from heaven. Behold, I give you authority to tread on serpents and scorpions, and over all the power of the enemy. Nothing will in any way hurt you. Nevertheless, don't rejoice in this, that the spirits are subject to you, but rejoice that your names are written in heaven."

Luke 10: 1 – 12, 17 – 20

Behold, a certain lawyer stood up and tested him, saying, "Teacher, what shall I do to inherit eternal life?"

He said to him, "What is written in the law? How do you read it?"

He answered, "You shall love the Lord your God with all your heart, with all your soul, with all your strength, and with all your mind; and your neighbor as yourself."

He said to him, "You have answered correctly. Do this, and you will live."

But he, desiring to justify himself, asked Jesus, "Who is my neighbor?"

Jesus answered, "A certain man was going down from Jerusalem to Jericho, and he fell among robbers, who both stripped him and beat him, and departed, leaving him half dead. By chance a certain priest was going down that way. When he saw him, he passed by on the other side. In the same way a Levite also, when he came to the place, and saw him, passed by on the other side. But a certain Samaritan, as he traveled, came where he was. When he saw him, he was moved with compassion, came to him, and bound up his wounds, pouring on oil and wine. He set him on his own animal, brought him to an inn, and took care of him. On the next day, when he departed, he took out two denarii, gave them to the host, and said to him, 'Take care of him. Whatever you spend beyond that, I will repay you when I return.' Now which of these three do you think seemed to be a neighbor to him who fell among the robbers?"

He said, "He who showed mercy on him."

Luke 10: 25 – 37

Sunday, July 17th, 2022

As they went on their way, he entered into a certain village, and a certain woman named Martha received him into her house. She had a sister called Mary, who also sat at Jesus' feet, and heard his word. But Martha was distracted with much serving, and she came up to him, and said, "Lord, don't you care that my sister left me to serve alone? Ask her therefore to help me."

Jesus answered her, "Martha, Martha, you are anxious and troubled about many things, but one thing is needed. Mary has chosen the good part, which will not be taken away from her."

Luke 10: 38 – 42

When he finished praying in a certain place, one of his disciples said to him, "Lord, teach us to pray, just as John also taught his disciples."

He said to them, "When you pray, say,

'Our Father in heaven,
may your name be kept holy.
May your Kingdom come.
May your will be done on earth, as it is in heaven.
Give us day by day our daily bread.
Forgive us our sins,
for we ourselves also forgive everyone who is indebted to us.
Bring us not into temptation,
but deliver us from the evil one.'"

He said to them, "Which of you, if you go to a friend at midnight, and tell him, 'Friend, lend me three loaves of bread, for a friend of mine has come to me from a journey, and I have nothing to set before him,' and he from within will answer and say, 'Don't bother me. The door is now shut, and my children are with me in bed. I can't get up and give it to you'? I tell you, although he will not rise and give it to him because he is his friend, yet because of his persistence, he will get up and give him as many as he needs.

"I tell you, keep asking, and it will be given you. Keep seeking, and you will find. Keep knocking, and it will be opened to you. For everyone who asks receives. He who seeks finds. To him who knocks it will be opened.

"Which of you fathers, if your son asks for bread, will give him a stone? Or if he asks for a fish, he won't give him a snake instead of a fish, will he? Or if he asks for an egg, he won't give him a scorpion, will he? If you then, being evil, know how to give good gifts to your children, how much more will your heavenly Father give the Holy Spirit to those who ask him?"

Luke 11: 1 – 13

One of the multitude said to him, "Teacher, tell my brother to divide the inheritance with me."

But he said to him, "Man, who made me a judge or an arbitrator over you?" He said to them, "Beware! Keep yourselves from covetousness, for a man's life doesn't consist of the abundance of the things which he possesses."

He spoke a parable to them, saying, "The ground of a certain rich man produced abundantly. He reasoned within himself, saying, 'What will I do, because I don't have room to store my crops?' He said, 'This is what I will do. I will pull down my barns, build bigger ones, and there I will store all my grain and my goods. I will tell my soul, "Soul, you have many goods laid up for many years. Take your ease, eat, drink, and be merry."'

"But God said to him, 'You foolish one, tonight your soul is required of you. The things which you have prepared—whose will they be?' So is he who lays up treasure for himself, and is not rich toward God."

Luke 12: 13 – 21

87

August

Don't be afraid, little flock, for it is your Father's good pleasure to give you the Kingdom. Sell that which you have, and give gifts to the needy. Make for yourselves purses which don't grow old, a treasure in the heavens that doesn't fail, where no thief approaches, neither moth destroys. For where your treasure is, there will your heart be also.

"Let your waist be dressed and your lamps burning. Be like men watching for their lord, when he returns from the wedding feast; that when he comes and knocks, they may immediately open to him. Blessed are those servants whom the lord will find watching when he comes. Most certainly I tell you that he will dress himself, make them recline, and will come and serve them. They will be blessed if he comes in the second or third watch, and finds them so. But know this, that if the master of the house had known in what hour the thief was coming, he would have watched, and not allowed his house to be broken into. Therefore be ready also, for the Son of Man is coming in an hour that you don't expect him."

Peter said to him, "Lord, are you telling this parable to us, or to everybody?"

The Lord said, "Who then is the faithful and wise steward, whom his lord will set over his household, to give them their portion of food at the right times? Blessed is that servant whom his lord will find doing so when he comes. Truly I tell you, that he will set him over all that he has. But if that servant says in his heart, 'My lord delays his coming,' and begins to beat the menservants and the maidservants, and to eat and drink, and to be drunken, then the lord of that servant will come in a day when he isn't expecting him, and in an hour that he doesn't know, and will cut him in two, and place his portion with the unfaithful. That servant, who knew his lord's will, and didn't prepare, nor do what he wanted, will be beaten with many stripes, but he who didn't know, and did things worthy of stripes, will be beaten with few stripes. To whomever much is given, of him will much be required; and to whom much was entrusted, of him more will be asked.

Luke 12: 32 – 48

"I came to throw fire on the earth. I wish it were already kindled. But I have a baptism to be baptized with, and how distressed I am until it is accomplished! Do you think that I have come to give peace in the earth? I tell you, no, but rather division. For from now on, there will be five in one house divided, three against two, and two against three. They will be divided, father against son, and son against father; mother against daughter, and daughter against her mother; mother-in-law against her daughter-in-law, and daughter-in-law against her mother-in-law."

Luke 12: 49 – 53

He went on his way through cities and villages, teaching, and traveling on to Jerusalem. One said to him, "Lord, are they few who are saved?"

He said to them, "Strive to enter in by the narrow door, for many, I tell you, will seek to enter in and will not be able. When once the master of the house has risen up, and has shut the door, and you begin to stand outside and to knock at the door, saying, 'Lord, Lord, open to us!' then he will answer and tell you, 'I don't know you or where you come from.' Then you will begin to say, 'We ate and drank in your presence, and you taught in our streets.' He will say, 'I tell you, I don't know where you come from. Depart from me, all you workers of iniquity.' There will be weeping and gnashing of teeth when you see Abraham, Isaac, Jacob, and all the prophets in God's Kingdom, and yourselves being thrown outside. They will come from the east, west, north, and south, and will sit down in God's Kingdom. Behold, there are some who are last who will be first, and there are some who are first who will be last."

Luke 13: 22 – 30

Sunday, August 28th, 2022

He spoke a parable to those who were invited, when he noticed how they chose the best seats, and said to them, "When you are invited by anyone to a wedding feast, don't sit in the best seat, since perhaps someone more honorable than you might be invited by him, and he who invited both of you would come and tell you, 'Make room for this person.' Then you would begin, with shame, to take the lowest place. But when you are invited, go and sit in the lowest place, so that when he who invited you comes, he may tell you, 'Friend, move up higher.' Then you will be honored in the presence of all who sit at the table with you. For everyone who exalts himself will be humbled, and whoever humbles himself will be exalted."

He also said to the one who had invited him, "When you make a dinner or a supper, don't call your friends, nor your brothers, nor your kinsmen, nor rich neighbors, or perhaps they might also return the favor, and pay you back. But when you make a feast, ask the poor, the maimed, the lame, or the blind; and you will be blessed, because they don't have the resources to repay you. For you will be repaid in the resurrection of the righteous."

Luke 14: 1, 7 – 14

September

Sunday, September 4th, 2022

Now great multitudes were going with him. He turned and said to them, "If anyone comes to me, and doesn't disregard his own father, mother, wife, children, brothers, and sisters, yes, and his own life also, he can't be my disciple. Whoever doesn't bear his own cross, and come after me, can't be my disciple. For which of you, desiring to build a tower, doesn't first sit down and count the cost, to see if he has enough to complete it? Or perhaps, when he has laid a foundation, and is not able to finish, everyone who sees begins to mock him, saying, 'This man began to build, and wasn't able to finish.' Or what king, as he goes to encounter another king in war, will not sit down first and consider whether he is able with ten thousand to meet him who comes against him with twenty thousand? Or else, while the other is yet a great way off, he sends an envoy, and asks for conditions of peace. So therefore whoever of you who doesn't renounce all that he has, he can't be my disciple.

Luke 14: 25 – 33

Sunday, September 11th, 2022

Now all the tax collectors and sinners were coming close to him to hear him. The Pharisees and the scribes murmured, saying, "This man welcomes sinners, and eats with them."

He told them this parable. "Which of you men, if you had one hundred sheep, and lost one of them, wouldn't leave the ninety-nine in the wilderness, and go after the one that was lost, until he found it? When he has found it, he carries it on his shoulders, rejoicing. When he comes home, he calls together his friends and his neighbors, saying to them, 'Rejoice with me, for I have found my sheep which was lost!' I tell you that even so there will be more joy in heaven over one sinner who repents, than over ninety-nine righteous people who need no repentance. Or what woman, if she had ten drachma coins, if she lost one drachma coin, wouldn't light a lamp, sweep the house, and seek diligently until she found it? When she has found it, she calls together her friends and neighbors, saying, 'Rejoice with me, for I have found the drachma which I had lost.' Even so, I tell you, there is joy in the presence of the angels of God over one sinner repenting."

He said, "A certain man had two sons. The younger of them said to his father, 'Father, give me my share of your property.' So he divided his livelihood between them. Not many days after, the younger son gathered all of this together and traveled into a far

97

country. There he wasted his property with riotous living. When he had spent all of it, there arose a severe famine in that country, and he began to be in need. He went and joined himself to one of the citizens of that country, and he sent him into his fields to feed pigs. He wanted to fill his belly with the husks that the pigs ate, but no one gave him any. But when he came to himself he said, 'How many hired servants of my father's have bread enough to spare, and I'm dying with hunger! I will get up and go to my father, and will tell him, "Father, I have sinned against heaven, and in your sight. I am no more worthy to be called your son. Make me as one of your hired servants."'

"He arose, and came to his father. But while he was still far off, his father saw him, and was moved with compassion, and ran, and fell on his neck, and kissed him. The son said to him, 'Father, I have sinned against heaven and in your sight. I am no longer worthy to be called your son.'

"But the father said to his servants, 'Bring out the best robe, and put it on him. Put a ring on his hand, and sandals on his feet. Bring the fattened calf, kill it, and let's eat, and celebrate; for this, my son, was dead, and is alive again. He was lost, and is found.' Then they began to celebrate.

"Now his elder son was in the field. As he came near to the house, he heard music and dancing. He called one of the servants to him, and asked what was going on. He said to him,

'Your brother has come, and your father has killed the fattened calf, because he has received him back safe and healthy.' But he was angry, and would not go in. Therefore his father came out, and begged him. But he answered his father, 'Behold, these many years I have served you, and I never disobeyed a commandment of yours, but you never gave me a goat, that I might celebrate with my friends. But when this your son came, who has devoured your living with prostitutes, you killed the fattened calf for him.'

"He said to him, 'Son, you are always with me, and all that is mine is yours. But it was appropriate to celebrate and be glad, for this, your brother, was dead, and is alive again. He was lost, and is found.'"

Luke 15: 1 – 32

He also said to his disciples, "There was a certain rich man who had a manager. An accusation was made to him that this man was wasting his possessions. He called him, and said to him, 'What is this that I hear about you? Give an accounting of your management, for you can no longer be manager.'

"The manager said within himself, 'What will I do, seeing that my lord is taking away the management position from me? I don't have strength to dig. I am ashamed to beg. I know what I will do, so that when I am removed from management, they may receive me into their houses.' Calling each one of his lord's debtors to him, he said to the first, 'How much do you owe to my lord?' He said, 'A hundred batos of oil.' He said to him, 'Take your bill, and sit down quickly and write fifty.' Then he said to another, 'How much do you owe?' He said, 'A hundred cors of wheat.' He said to him, 'Take your bill, and write eighty.'

"His lord commended the dishonest manager because he had done wisely, for the children of this world are, in their own generation, wiser than the children of the light. I tell you, make for yourselves friends by means of unrighteous mammon, so that when you fail, they may receive you into the eternal tents. He who is faithful in a very little is faithful also in much. He who is dishonest in a very little is also dishonest in much. If therefore you have not been faithful in the unrighteous mammon, who will commit to your trust the true riches? If you have not been faithful in that which is another's, who will give you that which is your own? No servant can serve two masters, for either he will hate the one, and love the other; or else he will hold to one, and despise the other. You aren't able to serve God and Mammon.

Luke 16: 1 – 13

"Now there was a certain rich man, and he was clothed in purple and fine linen, living in luxury every day. A certain beggar, named Lazarus, was taken to his gate, full of sores, and desiring to be fed with the crumbs that fell from the rich man's table. Yes, even the dogs came and licked his sores. The beggar died, and he was carried away by the angels to Abraham's bosom. The rich man also died, and was buried. In Hades, he lifted up his eyes, being in torment, and saw Abraham far off, and Lazarus at his bosom. He cried and said, 'Father Abraham, have mercy on me, and send Lazarus, that he may dip the tip of his finger in water, and cool my tongue! For I am in anguish in this flame.'

"But Abraham said, 'Son, remember that you, in your lifetime, received your good things, and Lazarus, in the same way, bad things. But here he is now comforted, and you are in anguish. Besides all this, between us and you there is a great gulf fixed, that those who want to pass from here to you are not able, and that no one may cross over from there to us.'

"He said, 'I ask you therefore, father, that you would send him to my father's house; for I have five brothers, that he may testify to them, so they won't also come into this place of torment.'

"But Abraham said to him, 'They have Moses and the prophets. Let them listen to them.'

"He said, 'No, father Abraham, but if one goes to them from the dead, they will repent.'

"He said to him, 'If they don't listen to Moses and the prophets, neither will they be persuaded if one rises from the dead.'"

Luke 16: 19 – 31

October

The apostles said to the Lord, "Increase our faith."

The Lord said, "If you had faith like a grain of mustard seed, you would tell this sycamore tree, 'Be uprooted, and be planted in the sea,' and it would obey you. But who is there among you, having a servant plowing or keeping sheep, that will say when he comes in from the field, 'Come immediately and sit down at the table,' and will not rather tell him, 'Prepare my supper, clothe yourself properly, and serve me, while I eat and drink. Afterward you shall eat and drink'? Does he thank that servant because he did the things that were commanded? I think not. Even so you also, when you have done all the things that are commanded you, say, 'We are unworthy servants. We have done our duty.'"

Luke 17: 5 – 10

As he was on his way to Jerusalem, he was passing along the borders of Samaria and Galilee. As he entered into a certain village, ten men who were lepers met him, who stood at a distance. They lifted up their voices, saying, "Jesus, Master, have mercy on us!"

When he saw them, he said to them, "Go and show yourselves to the priests." As they went, they were cleansed. One of them, when he saw that he was healed, turned back, glorifying God with a loud voice. He fell on his face at Jesus' feet, giving him thanks; and he was a Samaritan. Jesus answered, "Weren't the ten cleansed? But where are the nine? Were there none found who returned to give glory to God, except this foreigner?" Then he said to him, "Get up, and go your way. Your faith has healed you."

Luke 17: 11 – 19

He also spoke a parable to them that they must always pray, and not give up, saying, "There was a judge in a certain city who didn't fear God, and didn't respect man. A widow was in that city, and she often came to him, saying, 'Defend me from my adversary!' He wouldn't for a while, but afterward he said to himself, 'Though I neither fear God, nor respect man, yet because this widow bothers me, I will defend her, or else she will wear me out by her continual coming.'"

The Lord said, "Listen to what the unrighteous judge says. Won't God avenge his chosen ones who are crying out to him day and night, and yet he exercises patience with them? I tell you that he will avenge them quickly. Nevertheless, when the Son of Man comes, will he find faith on the earth?"

Luke 18: 1 – 8

He also spoke this parable to certain people who were convinced of their own righteousness, and who despised all others. "Two men went up into the temple to pray; one was a Pharisee, and the other was a tax collector. The Pharisee stood and prayed to himself like this: 'God, I thank you that I am not like the rest of men, extortionists, unrighteous, adulterers, or even like this tax collector. I fast twice a week. I give tithes of all that I get.' But the tax collector, standing far away, wouldn't even lift up his eyes to heaven, but beat his breast, saying, 'God, be merciful to me, a sinner!' I tell you, this man went down to his house justified rather than the other; for everyone who exalts himself will be humbled, but he who humbles himself will be exalted."

Luke 18: 9 – 14

He entered and was passing through Jericho. There was a man named Zacchaeus. He was a chief tax collector, and he was rich. He was trying to see who Jesus was, and couldn't because of the crowd, because he was short. He ran on ahead, and climbed up into a sycamore tree to see him, for he was going to pass that way. When Jesus came to the place, he looked up and saw him, and said to him, "Zacchaeus, hurry and come down, for today I must stay at your house." He hurried, came down, and received him joyfully. When they saw it, they all murmured, saying, "He has gone in to lodge with a man who is a sinner."

Zacchaeus stood and said to the Lord, "Behold, Lord, half of my goods I give to the poor. If I have wrongfully exacted anything of anyone, I restore four times as much."

Jesus said to him, "Today, salvation has come to this house, because he also is a son of Abraham. For the Son of Man came to seek and to save that which was lost."

Luke 19: 1 – 10

November

Some of the Sadducees came to him, those who deny that there is a resurrection. They asked him, "Teacher, Moses wrote to us that if a man's brother dies having a wife, and he is childless, his brother should take the wife and raise up children for his brother. There were therefore seven brothers. The first took a wife, and died childless. The second took her as wife, and he died childless. The third took her, and likewise the seven all left no children, and died. Afterward the woman also died. Therefore in the resurrection whose wife of them will she be? For the seven had her as a wife."

Jesus said to them, "The children of this age marry, and are given in marriage. But those who are considered worthy to attain to that age and the resurrection from the dead neither marry nor are given in marriage. For they can't die any more, for they are like the angels, and are children of God, being children of the resurrection. But that the dead are raised, even Moses showed at the bush, when he called the Lord 'The God of Abraham, the God of Isaac, and the God of Jacob.' Now he is not the God of the dead, but of the living, for all are alive to him."

Luke 20: 27 – 38

Sunday, November 13th, 2022

As some were talking about the temple and how it was decorated with beautiful stones and gifts, he said, "As for these things which you see, the days will come, in which there will not be left here one stone on another that will not be thrown down."

They asked him, "Teacher, so when will these things be? What is the sign that these things are about to happen?"

He said, "Watch out that you don't get led astray, for many will come in my name, saying, 'I am he,' and, 'The time is at hand.' Therefore don't follow them. When you hear of wars and disturbances, don't be terrified, for these things must happen first, but the end won't come immediately."

Then he said to them, "Nation will rise against nation, and kingdom against kingdom. There will be great earthquakes, famines, and plagues in various places. There will be terrors and great signs from heaven. But before all these things, they will lay their hands on you and will persecute you, delivering you up to synagogues and prisons, bringing you before kings and governors for my name's sake. It will turn out as a testimony for you. Settle it therefore in your hearts not to meditate beforehand how to answer, for I will give you a mouth and wisdom which all your adversaries will not be able to withstand or to contradict. You will be handed over even by parents, brothers, relatives, and friends. They will cause some of you to be put to death. You will be hated by all men for my name's sake. And not a hair of your head will perish.

"By your endurance you will win your lives.

Luke 21: 5 – 19

The people stood watching. The rulers with them also scoffed at him, saying, "He saved others. Let him save himself, if this is the Christ of God, his chosen one!"

The soldiers also mocked him, coming to him and offering him vinegar, and saying, "If you are the King of the Jews, save yourself!"

An inscription was also written over him in letters of Greek, Latin, and Hebrew: "THIS IS THE KING OF THE JEWS."

One of the criminals who was hanged insulted him, saying, "If you are the Christ, save yourself and us!"

But the other answered, and rebuking him said, "Don't you even fear God, seeing you are under the same condemnation? And we indeed justly, for we receive the due reward for our deeds, but this man has done nothing wrong." He said to Jesus, "Lord, remember me when you come into your Kingdom."

Jesus said to him, "Assuredly I tell you, today you will be with me in Paradise."

Luke 23: 35 – 43

Sunday, November 27th, 2022
First Sunday of Advent

As the days of Noah were, so will the coming of the Son of Man be. For as in those days which were before the flood they were eating and drinking, marrying and giving in marriage, until the day that Noah entered into the ship, and they didn't know until the flood came and took them all away, so will the coming of the Son of Man be. Then two men will be in the field: one will be taken and one will be left. Two women will be grinding at the mill: one will be taken and one will be left. Watch therefore, for you don't know in what hour your Lord comes. But know this, that if the master of the house had known in what watch of the night the thief was coming, he would have watched, and would not have allowed his house to be broken into. Therefore also be ready, for in an hour that you don't expect, the Son of Man will come.

Matthew 24: 37 – 44

December

Sunday, December 4ᵗʰ, 2022
Second Sunday of Advent

In those days, John the Baptizer came, preaching in the wilderness of Judea, saying, "Repent, for the Kingdom of Heaven is at hand!" For this is he who was spoken of by Isaiah the prophet, saying,

"The voice of one crying in the wilderness,
make the way of the Lord ready!
Make his paths straight!"

Now John himself wore clothing made of camel's hair with a leather belt around his waist. His food was locusts and wild honey. Then people from Jerusalem, all of Judea, and all the region around the Jordan went out to him. They were baptized by him in the Jordan, confessing their sins.

But when he saw many of the Pharisees and Sadducees coming for his baptism, he said to them, "You offspring of vipers, who warned you to flee from the wrath to come? Therefore produce fruit worthy of repentance! Don't think to yourselves, 'We have Abraham for our father,' for I tell you that God is able to raise up children to Abraham from these stones. Even now the ax lies at the root of the trees. Therefore every tree that doesn't produce good fruit is cut down, and cast into the fire.

"I indeed baptize you in water for repentance, but he who comes after me is mightier than I, whose sandals I am not worthy to carry. He will baptize you in the Holy Spirit. His winnowing fork is in his hand, and he will thoroughly cleanse his threshing floor. He will gather his wheat into the barn, but the chaff he will burn up with unquenchable fire."

Matthew 3: 1 – 12

Thursday, 8th, 2022

The Immaculate Conception of the Blessed Virgin Mary

Now in the sixth month, the angel Gabriel was sent from God to a city of Galilee named Nazareth, to a virgin pledged to be married to a man whose name was Joseph, of David's house. The virgin's name was Mary. Having come in, the angel said to her, "Rejoice, you highly favored one! The Lord is with you. Blessed are you among women!"

But when she saw him, she was greatly troubled at the saying, and considered what kind of salutation this might be. The angel said to her, "Don't be afraid, Mary, for you have found favor with God. Behold, you will conceive in your womb and give birth to a son, and shall name him 'Jesus.' He will be great and will be called the Son of the Most High. The Lord God will give him the throne of his father David, and he will reign over the house of Jacob forever. There will be no end to his Kingdom."

Mary said to the angel, "How can this be, seeing I am a virgin?"

The angel answered her, "The Holy Spirit will come on you, and the power of the Most High will overshadow you. Therefore also the holy one who is born from you will be called the Son of God. Behold, Elizabeth your relative also has conceived a son in her old age; and this is the sixth month with her who was called barren. For nothing spoken by God is impossible."

Mary said, "Behold, the servant of the Lord; let it be done to me according to your word."

Luke 1: 26 – 38

Sunday, December 11ᵗʰ, 2022
Third Sunday of Advent

Now when John heard in the prison the works of Christ, he sent two of his disciples and said to him, "Are you he who comes, or should we look for another?"

Jesus answered them, "Go and tell John the things which you hear and see: the blind receive their sight, the lame walk, the lepers are cleansed, the deaf hear, the dead are raised up, and the poor have good news preached to them. Blessed is he who finds no occasion for stumbling in me."

As these went their way, Jesus began to say to the multitudes concerning John, "What did you go out into the wilderness to see? A reed shaken by the wind? But what did you go out to see? A man in soft clothing? Behold, those who wear soft clothing are in kings' houses. But why did you go out? To see a prophet? Yes, I tell you, and much more than a prophet. For this is he, of whom it is written, 'Behold, I send my messenger before your face, who will prepare your way before you.' Most certainly I tell you, among those who are born of women there has not arisen anyone greater than John the Baptizer; yet he who is least in the Kingdom of Heaven is greater than he.

Matthew 11: 2 – 11

122

Sunday, December 18th, 2022
Fourth Sunday of Advent

Now the birth of Jesus Christ was like this: After his mother, Mary, was engaged to Joseph, before they came together, she was found pregnant by the Holy Spirit. Joseph, her husband, being a righteous man, and not willing to make her a public example, intended to put her away secretly. But when he thought about these things, behold, an angel of the Lord appeared to him in a dream, saying, "Joseph, son of David, don't be afraid to take to yourself Mary as your wife, for that which is conceived in her is of the Holy Spirit. She shall give birth to a son. You shall name him Jesus, for it is he who shall save his people from their sins."

Now all this has happened that it might be fulfilled which was spoken by the Lord through the prophet, saying,

"Behold, the virgin shall be with child,
and shall give birth to a son.
They shall call his name Immanuel,"
which is, being interpreted, "God with us."

Joseph arose from his sleep, and did as the angel of the Lord commanded him, and took his wife to himself;

Matthew 1: 18 – 24

123

Saturday, December 24th, 2022
Christmas Eve

Now in those days, a decree went out from Caesar Augustus that all the world should be enrolled. This was the first enrollment made when Quirinius was governor of Syria. All went to enroll themselves, everyone to his own city. Joseph also went up from Galilee, out of the city of Nazareth, into Judea, to David's city, which is called Bethlehem, because he was of the house and family of David; to enroll himself with Mary, who was pledged to be married to him as wife, being pregnant.

While they were there, the day had come for her to give birth. She gave birth to her firstborn son. She wrapped him in bands of cloth, and laid him in a feeding trough, because there was no room for them in the inn. There were shepherds in the same country staying in the field, and keeping watch by night over their flock. Behold, an angel of the Lord stood by them, and the glory of the Lord shone around them, and they were terrified. The angel said to them, "Don't be afraid, for behold, I bring you good news of great joy which will be to all the people. For there is born to you today, in David's city, a Savior, who is Christ the Lord. This is the sign to you: you will find a baby wrapped in strips of cloth, lying in a feeding trough." Suddenly, there was with the angel a multitude of the heavenly army praising God, and saying,

"Glory to God in the highest, on earth peace, good will toward men."

Luke 2: 1 – 14

Sunday, December 25th, 2022
Christmas, The Nativity of the Lord

In the beginning was the Word, and the Word was with God, and the Word was God. The same was in the beginning with God. All things were made through him. Without him, nothing was made that has been made. In him was life, and the life was the light of men. The light shines in the darkness, and the darkness hasn't overcome it. There came a man, sent from God, whose name was John. The same came as a witness, that he might testify about the light, that all might believe through him. He was not the light, but was sent that he might testify about the light. The true light that enlightens everyone was coming into the world.

He was in the world, and the world was made through him, and the world didn't recognize him. He came to his own, and those who were his own didn't receive him. But as many as received him, to them he gave the right to become God's children, to those who believe in his name: who were born not of blood, nor of the will of the flesh, nor of the will of man, but of God. The Word became flesh, and lived among us. We saw his glory, such glory as of the one and only Son of the Father, full of grace and truth. John testified about him. He cried out, saying, "This was he of whom I said, 'He who comes after me has surpassed me, for he was before me.'" From his fullness we all received grace upon grace. For the law was given through Moses. Grace and truth were realized through Jesus Christ. No one has seen God at any time. The one and only Son, who is in the bosom of the Father, has declared him.

John 1, 1 -18

Friday, December 30th, 2022
The Holy Family

Now when they had departed, behold, an angel of the Lord appeared to Joseph in a dream, saying, "Arise and take the young child and his mother, and flee into Egypt, and stay there until I tell you, for Herod will seek the young child to destroy him."

He arose and took the young child and his mother by night and departed into Egypt, and was there until the death of Herod, that it might be fulfilled which was spoken by the Lord through the prophet, saying, "Out of Egypt I called my son."

(...)

But when Herod was dead, behold, an angel of the Lord appeared in a dream to Joseph in Egypt, saying, "Arise and take the young child and his mother, and go into the land of Israel, for those who sought the young child's life are dead."

He arose and took the young child and his mother, and came into the land of Israel. But when he heard that Archelaus was reigning over Judea in the place of his father, Herod, he was afraid to go there. Being warned in a dream, he withdrew into the region of Galilee, and came and lived in a city called Nazareth; that it might be fulfilled which was spoken through the prophets that he will be called a Nazarene.

Matthew 2: 13 – 15, 19 – 23

128

Saturday, December 31st, 2022
Saint Sylvester

In the beginning was the Word, and the Word was with God, and the Word was God. The same was in the beginning with God. All things were made through him. Without him, nothing was made that has been made. In him was life, and the life was the light of men. The light shines in the darkness, and the darkness hasn't overcome it. There came a man, sent from God, whose name was John. The same came as a witness, that he might testify about the light, that all might believe through him. He was not the light, but was sent that he might testify about the light. The true light that enlightens everyone was coming into the world.

He was in the world, and the world was made through him, and the world didn't recognize him. He came to his own, and those who were his own didn't receive him. But as many as received him, to them he gave the right to become God's children, to those who believe in his name: who were born not of blood, nor of the will of the flesh, nor of the will of man, but of God. The Word became flesh, and lived among us. We saw his glory, such glory as of the one and only Son of the Father, full of grace and truth. John testified about him. He cried out, saying, "This was he of whom I said, 'He who comes after me has surpassed me, for he was before me.'" From his fullness we all received grace upon grace. For the law was given through Moses. Grace and truth were realized through Jesus Christ. No one has seen God at any time. The one and only Son, who is in the bosom of the Father, has declared him.

John 1: 1 – 18

Important Prayers

Ave Maria

Ave Maria, gratia plena,
Dominus tecum.
Benedicta tu in mulieribus,
et benedictus fructus ventris tui, Iesus.

Sancta Maria, Mater Dei,
ora pro nobis peccatoribus
nunc et in hora mortis nostrae.

Amen.

Hail Mary

Hail Mary, full of grace,
the Lord is with thee.
Blessed art thou amongst women,
and blessed is the fruit of thy womb, Jesus.

Holy Mary, Mother of God,
pray for us sinners,
now and at the hour of our death.

Amen.

Pater Noster

Pater Noster,

qui es in caelis,

sanctificetur nomen tuum.

Adveniat regnum tuum.

Fiat voluntas tua, sicut in caelo, et in terra.

Panem nostrum quotidianum da nobis hodie.

Et dimitte nobis debita nostra,

sicut et nos dimittimus debitoribus nostris.

Et ne nos inducas in tentationem:

sed libera nos a malo.

Quia tuum est regnum et potestas et Gloria in saecula.

Amen.

Our Father

Our Father, who art in heaven,
Hallowed be thy Name. Thy kingdom come.
Thy will be done, On earth as it is in heaven.
Give us this day our daily bread. And forgive us our trespasses,
As we forgive those who trespass against us.
And lead us not into temptation,
But deliver us from evil.
For thine is the kingdom, and the power,
and the glory, for ever and ever.

Amen.

Credo

Credo in deum patrem omnipotentem,
creatorem coeli et terrae;

Et in Iesum Christum,
filium eius unicum,
dominum nostrum,
qui conceptus est de Spiritu sancto,
natus ex Maria virgine,
passus sub Pontio Pilato,
crucifixus, mortuus et sepultus,
descendit ad inferna,
tertia die resurrexit a mortuis,
ascendit ad coelos,
sedet ad dexteram dei patris omnipotentis,
inde venturus est iudicare vivos et mortuos;

Credo in Spiritum sanctum,
sanctam ecclesiam catholicam,
sanctorum communionem,
remissionem peccatorum,
carnis resurrectionem,
et vitam aeternam.

Amen.

The Creed

I believe in God, the Father almighty,
creator of heaven and earth.

I believe in Jesus Christ, his only Son, our Lord.
He was conceived by the power of the Holy Spirit
and born of the Virgin Mary.
He suffered under Pontius Pilate,
was crucified, died, and was buried.
He descended to the dead.
On the third day he rose again.
He ascended into heaven,
and is seated at the right hand of the Father.
He will come again to judge the living and the dead.

I believe in the Holy Spirit,
the holy catholic Church,
the communion of saints,
the forgiveness of sins,
the resurrection of the body,
and the life everlasting.

Amen.

Confiteor

Confiteor Deo omnipotenti
et vobis, fratres,
quia peccavi nimis
cogitatione, verbo, opere et omissione:
mea culpa, mea culpa, mea maxima culpa.
Ideo precor beatam Mariam semper Virginem,
omnes Angelos et Sanctos,
et vos, fratres,
orare pro me ad Dominum Deum nostrum.

Confiteor

I confess to almighty God
and to you, my brothers and sisters,
that I have greatly sinned,
in my thoughts and in my words,
in what I have done and in what I have failed to do,
through my fault, through my fault,
through my most grievous fault;
therefore I ask blessed Mary ever-Virgin,
all the Angels and Saints,
and you, my brothers and sisters,
to pray for me to the Lord our God.

Non nobis Domine, non nobis,
sed nomini tuo da gloriam.

Psalm, 115: 1